Let My People Go

A. A. Allen

Must Have Books
503 Deerfield Place
Victoria, BC
V9B 6G5
Canada

ISBN 9781773237350

I make no apology for the Bible! I make no apology for the way people shout and praise God in these meetings. I make no apology for the loud noise of hundreds of people clapping their hands in praise! People shout, sing, and dance in the Spirit in these meetings.

I will not apologize for the way children of God who attend our meetings talk in tongues and prophesy! I have no apology for God's Word! I cannot apologize for what God declared we ought to be receiving and enjoying today!

The cold, dead, dry modern preacher, bound by religious tradition, will never know or experience this NEW RESTORATION REVIVAL! He is satisfied with form and ceremony and dead ritual. Should this revival happen to break out in his church, he would apologize for it and try to make light of it because he does not know anything about it! He has never had Revival! He is ashamed of revival and does not want it. What people feel in these revival services is just a portion of the outpouring of God's Spirit.

REAL MIRACLE RESTORATION REVIVAL CAN NEVER TAKE PLACE IN ANY
COUNTRY UNTIL TRADITION IS BROKEN DOWN!

The Pharisees, (Mark 7:5) came running to the Lord, asking, "Why walk not thy disciples according to the tradition of the elders ?" Evidently, the Pharisees, Sadducees and the religious leaders did not like the way the disciples were following the Lord. These leaders were angry because they had broken away from the TRADITION OF THE ELDERS, and refused to follow their man-made tradition. And, in fact, those religious hypocrites did not like the way Jesus was failing to conform to the tradition of their time. Christ did not conform to the tradition of their community or their church. So, they came to Him with a question, "Why is it that your disciples have broken away, and no longer follow the tradition of the elders ?"

Do you remember what Jesus said? His reply is still appropriate now for the people of this country! This is what it will take for Revival to break through here because there are too many Church people who are bound by mere, plain tradition. Tradition, which Jesus said,

"Makes of none effect the commandments of God!"

This is what Christ said, "You are fine teachers to cancel what God commanded, in order to keep what men have handed down." (Mark 7: 8) William's Translation)

"You have a fine way of rejecting thus thwarting and nullifying and doing away with the commandment of God in order to keep your tradition - your own human regulations." (V. 8

Amplified) "You neglect God's commandment: you hold fast to men's traditions." (V. 8 Weymouth "Repealing the Word of God in the interests of the tradition which you keep up." (Mark 7:13 Moffatt)

"Politely you frustrate the law of God . . . you neutralize God's Word ..." (Berkeley)

"Canceling the Word of God..." .(Rotherham) "You do injustice to the commandment of God so as to sustain your own tradition ..." (V. 9) "So you dishonor the Word of God for the sake of tradition ..." (V. 13 Lamsa) "You are clever in making God's commandments of no account, but your tradition must be observed." (Norlie) "Why is it that your disciples do not follow the tradition of the elders?" Jesus answered, "You are clever in your making God's commandments of no account, that your tradition might be observed!"

When those conformists came to Jesus, He had an answer! Many people coming to these meetings are wondering why we do not conform to the tradition of some of their elders in these cold, dead churches which were established in the 15th, 16th, 17th, 18th or even the 19th Century.

I would like to inform you that God is doing a NEW THING which He did not do in former times. We are living in the Twentieth Century! God said, "Behold, I'll do a new thing." God is doing something today that He has never done before.

Some of these elders (including Pentecostal) are preaching nothing but man-made, handed-down tradition. Some people who attend our meetings know nothing about God's Word, what God promised or what God is doing today. All they know are the tradition of men. Revival will never come to any country until men forget, break away from and refuse to follow, the tradition of men. When you break away. God can and will do something for you.

"A TRADITION is a belief or practice not derived directly from the Bible, but arising and handed down within the Christian community." (Webster's Unabridged) As it was with the Pharisees and Sadducees in Jesus' day, modern religious denominations have no Scripture to validate the existence of tradition. Yet, traditions are still practiced and are often considered before the Word of God.

Many people come into these meetings and are surprised and say, "Oh, this is so funny.

Why are these people acting this way? They certainly do not act this way in my church." It could be that the people in your church are following the tradition of the elders that have been handed down from the 18th Century. These nullify and make of none effect the Word and commandments of God!

One can stand in the pulpit and quote Scripture hour after hour and some people will say;

"Well, I know it is in the Bible, BUT it is not according to the Methodist Church, the Lutherans, the Baptists, the Presbyterians, the Anglican Church, *the Assemblies of God or the Church of God in Christ!"

It may not be according to your church, however, IT IS ACCORDING TO THE WORD

OF GOD! It is what God declared He would do in this day and hour.

One woman had an issue of blood. (Luke 8: 43) She had gone to all the doctors. The Bible states that she "... was nothing bettered, but rather grew worse,". (Mark 5:26) She had spent all of her money on physicians and yet she was not helped. Instead she grew worse. As long as she abode in her bondage, she grew worse and worse, more and more poor. Finally, she decided she would jump over the fence and get away from the tradition of the elders.

She would do something she would not be allowed to do in her church. She would press, fight and battle her way through until she touched the hem of His garment. She declared,

"If I can but touch the hem of His garment, I shall be made every whit whole." But according to the tradition of the elders, they would have said, "Oh, it's hysteria, it's hysteria!" Some of the newspapers, whose reporters see things happening in our meetings, call it "mass hysteria". They call it "mass-emotionalism".

If people are saved, healed and delivered; if actual miracles of great magnitude happen, where people are bettered; in all truth, it is GOD'S MIRACLE WORKING POWER!

This woman, desperate, began to push, shove and crowd her way through to Jesus. "Excuse me! Pardon me! I beg your pardon! Oh, I'm sorry 1 Sorry, but I have to get to Him! I must fight my way through! I must get to Him!"

Some say, "It's mass hysteria. You better stay away from those Allen Meetings. People get hysterical and push and push" and push toward God!

According to the tradition of the elders, everything should be done perfectly and calmly.

Let it be dignified and beautiful. Do not get excited! Do not show any emotion. If you do, the tradition of the church and the tradition of the cold, dead religious elders will make you out to be an extremist. They will call it sensationalism if you dare to do what Jesus did. He smeared a man's face with mud and spittle and then told him to go wash the mud from his eyes and come again seeing!

If Jesus stepped into some of these churches today and opened a casket, commanding that the dead be raised, people would call it sensationalism! BUT JESUS DID NOT GO INTO THE CHURCH WHEN HE WAS HERE ON EARTHI He waited until the funeral was over and the procession was in the middle of the main street in Nain. Then He cried,

"Halt!" Christ broke completely and entirely away from tradition. He did not do anything as the elders did. The elders were certainly never known for raising the dead! I'm not trying to be like the elders. I'm patterning my ministry after the Greatest Minister. He's in all our services. His name is Jesus! He opened the casket right out in public and commanded that the dead arise! Tradition would say, "If you MUST pray for the sick, you should do it in the quietness and seclusion of the prayer room! In order to save embarrassment, it should never be done sensationally or publicly. I wonder who would be embarrassed to get healed? Could it be to save the preacher's embarrassment, when they do not get healed ?

The apostle, Peter, was an extremist. He went a step further. Peter was really a sensationalist.

He marched past the sick and suffering in the streets of Jerusalem, neither touching anyone or anointing them with oil. He did not even lay hands on them. Talk about being sensational and breaking away from the tradition of the elders, Peter was doing just that!

He simply walked by and his shadow healed the sick and brought the miraculous!

Speaking of sensationalism, Christ went through doors, the doors being shut! He walked on the waters and the waters coagulated under His feet and supported Him! Christ did what none of the elders had ever done! The disciples began to shout and praise the Lord with a LOUD voice for all the things they had seen. They had really broken away from the tradition of the elders. They tore the limbs off the trees and put them in the path of a little donkey that Christ was riding so that it would not have to walk on the ground. They were even taking their coats off, making a path on the ground for the ass to walk on.

The tradition of the elders today would call it emotionalism or fanaticism. They've taken this thing to extremes!" or "It's sensationalism. The people have become hysterical! Why, they're tearing the palm boughs off the trees!"

One little woman pushed and shoved and said, "I must get to Him! If I can but touch the hem of His garment, I'll be made every whit whole!" You will never find people doing that in the modern church. They just come and sit, quietly dignified in their Sunday best, and have form, ceremony and ritual. The congregation listens to a religious lecture - an essay that appeals to man's intellect but never touches the soul or stirs the Spirit. There will never be revival in cold, dead, formalistic churches that nullify the effect of the commandments of God by following mere tradition of men! I'm not referring ONLY to these Methodists, Baptists, Presbyterian, Lutherans, Catholics or the Church of England; THE

PENTECOSTALS ARE BOUND BY TRADITION TOO! There are few sick being healed in these groups, even when they are brought for prayer. Few miracles are taking place because the ones that stand behind the sacred desks are bound by the tradition of men.

Jesus said, "... it makes of none effect the Word of God, or the commandments of God."

(Amplified) We can be so bound by tradition of men, customs that have been handed down in the community, until the Word of God does not mean a thing.

King David received such a great blessing from God, that he forgot all about the tradition of the elders. The power of God hit him and he danced before the Lord with all his might!

Michal, his wife, did not like it because it was not according to the tradition of the elders!

In sarcasm, she rebuked him. She despised him in her heart! She saw the manifestation of God in a man. It was not the works of the flesh! It was not emotionalism. It was not fanaticism. It was not hysteria. It was God's power upon a man. It was old-timed, heart-felt, religion.

Michal did not like it, for it is written, "... She despised him in her heart." (II Samuel 6:16) Why? Because it was not according to tradition. He strayed from tradition and let God do something for him. God cannot do anything for you until you break away from man-made, handed-down tradition. As long as you stay bound by the tradition of men, you cannot enjoy the blessing of God, neither will you have Revival with healing and miracles.

It is amazing how many Pentecostal preachers and followers in the world are so bound by tradition. If people shout and praise God, dance in the Spirit, even PENTECOSTAL

TRADITION will brand it hysteria or emotionalism . . . fanaticism. If we preach an old-fashioned sermon on hell-fire and against sin and make an altar call where people come running by the multitudes to be saved, drawn by a contrite spirit, tradition will say,

"It's mass psychology!" That is not what I call it! I call it the convicting power of the Holy Ghost! IT IS REVIVAL!

If you raise your hands, clap your hands, rejoice in God, make a joyful noise, praise Him on the instruments and organs, and use the kind of music we play, religious tradition will call it, "Rock and Roll" or say, "That's jazz!"

Cold, dead tradition says everything has to be formal and solemn. Why do these leaders say this? Tradition has never been born again! If tradition would ever get saved and have a change of heart, start obeying and observing the commandments of God, it would forget all this form and begin to enjoy the blessing of God.

Tradition will always oppose the moving of God's Spirit. This is one reason Revival can never come to the world until man-made tradition which nullifies and makes of none effect the commandments of God, is overcome.

Blind Bartimaeus sat by the roadside when he heard a crowd passing by. When that noise started, he realized that it could be Jesus. He had waited all his life for such an opportunity to have his eyes opened.

If he had followed the tradition of the elders, he would have sat quietly by the wayside saying, "Now the Lord knows my need. He knows that I am blind. He realizes that I want to be healed. This thing must be done decently and in order. It must be beautifully done in form because if I get emotional, it will be branded as of the devil." Not so! Instead Bartimaeus cried out! Now if he had followed the tradition of the elders, he would have sat quietly dignified and folded his hands and said, "Well, if it is the will of the Lord to heal me. He knows I'm here. He knows all things and he will stop." Not so! Bartimaeus cried out! He broke away from all tradition. The Bible declares, " ... he began to cry out, and say, Jesus, thou Son of David, have mercy on me." (Mark 10: 47) Jesus broke away from the tradition of the elders when he went to the tomb of Lazarus.

The Bible says, ". . .he cried with a loud voice, Lazarus, come forth." (John 11: 43) The Pharisees and Sadducees and religious leaders did not like it when they came into Jerusalem and they heard them shouting with a LOUD voice. They called the Master aside,

"... Master, rebuke thy disciples."

Why did they want Him to rebuke the disciples? Was it because they were making such a noise and throwing palm boughs in the road? No! It was because they had broken away from the tradition of the elders and were enjoying the blessing of God and seeing the miracles He performed. Jesus rebuked the elders, "... I tell you that, if these should hold their peace, (if these people did not make noise) the stones would immediately cry out."

(Luke 19:40) Thank God, some people were desperate enough to break away from the tradition of the elders and receive something from God.

Bartimaeus broke away and cried, "JESUS!" with a LOUD voice. Bartimaeus' eyes were opened only after he came out of the form and tradition of the elders.

In the book of Luke, a boy had been down in the hog pen. Having spent all he had on riotous living, he wound up in the hog pen eating swill with the pigs. Finally, he came to himself, crawled out of the hog pen and started back home. The father, meeting him halfway, put a robe on him, shoes on his feet, a ring on his finger and kissed him. "For this my son was dead, and is alive again; he was lost, and is found ..." (Luke 15: 24) The young man in contrition said, "I'm '. . . no more worthy to be called thy son: make me as one of thy hired servants.' " (Luke 15:19) The father took him into his house, which typifies the House of God.

The eldest son, who was still bound by the tradition of the elders, came up to the house and heard "music and dancing". He did not know a revival was in progress. He was so prejudiced, he could not discern what was going on.

He called one of the servants to ask him if he knew what was going on and what these things meant. I believe the servant must have asked, "Don't you know?" Of course he did not know. He was still bound by the tradition of the elders who believe that everything must be done quietly, in a dignified manner. The elder brother believed that people should never get emotional in church.

Many people that criticize these meetings often rite long letters to me and tell me they abhor, shudder at what they see in these meetings.

Why does it bother people so much to see others enjoying the blessings of God? One Pentecostal lady told me that she felt so ashamed to see other Pentecostal folk "carry on"

the way they do. A scripture in Proverbs caused her to feel ashamed again; "When pride cometh, then cometh shame ..." (Proverbs 11: 2) People do not criticize others for getting emotional at a football game or at a cricket or soccer game. When it is something outside the church, they call it "fun" or enthusiasm. I think more people should get enthusiastic about church. If it hurts these critical people so much, why do they keep coming back to the meetings ? Why don't they stay away ?

Why do they get so angry? When people see things they do not like which have nothing to do with church, they usually just go their way and forget it. Why do they get so angry at us? Could it be the devil in them who is getting angry?

How can revival ever come to a people when they brand genuine worship as "fanaticism" ?

How can God move in an atmosphere where the manifestations of the Spirit and power of God is called, "hysteria" ?

Can revival come to a place where the healing of the sick is degraded as being done "by the power of Satan" ? Can God come to a church that brands dancing in the Spirit, "fleshly"?

Can God bring revival to a church world that calls the old-fashioned preacher a "calamity howler"? Can God bring revival when His ministers are called "Sensationalists" and joyful Miracle Music is called "Rock 'n Roll"? What do you think? Traditions are responsible for these mockings of the real moving of God's power.

The Apostle Paul never had trouble with the traditionalistic elders until he refused to walk with them after their tradition. After he was converted and broke away from tradition, he found himself in prison being beaten, ridiculed, persecuted, hated, rejected, considered dung and the off-scouring of the earth. Please note that his MIRACLE MINISTRY ONLY

began when he was willing to forsake ALL for Christ. It was then, and then only, that he could heal the sick with the aprons from his body and the handkerchiefs from his pockets.

Paul even raised the dead!

How many preachers, like Phillip, does God have today? Most of the deacons, now, would not dare leave the church long enough to go to Samaria and stir the city with a Miracle Ministry. Pentecostal tradition today (refer to your church constitution and by-laws) would place poor Phillip and all the other deacons in the position of controlling the pastor and the church. However, Scripturally, it is not the duty of the deacons to see to it that the pastor adheres to all the doctrines, by-laws and unscriptural government of the modern church. If the deacons were not present in some churches, revival might break out!

People might break away from tradition and begin selling their possessions and goods and laying the money at the pastor's feet as they did in Bible days. If that happened, the deacons might not get to count the offerings and control spending.

Not many deacons are being "gnashed upon" by the teeth of the elders today as Stephen was for refusing to walk after their tradition. Revival in Stephen's soul set him aflame for God so that the religious elders who were listening ". . .were cut to the heart, and they gnashed on him with their teeth . . . and ran upon him with one accord, and cast him out of the city, and stoned him ..." (Acts 7: 54 - 58) Fear of persecution is the main reason that most preachers and church people adhere so closely to form, ritual, ceremony and religious tradition. Ministers are afraid of the elders, bishops, general overseers and the district and general superintendents. Some are fearful of having no ministry outside their denominational bondage. In God's sight, many have no ministry within denominations!

Christ was actually hated for His stand against denominational bondage. All His disciples in the early church suffered a violent death for taking their stand and following Jesus.

The followers of Christ today cannot expect to escape persecution and opposition from the same religious leaders.

Some people refer to their dead, cold, formalistic ritual as church. They would have to think this since they have never known anything else.

When they fight for their religious tradition, they may think sincerely that they are right in fighting. Christ called them "blind leaders of the blind". One can be blind, unsaved and even demon possessed and think he is doing God a favor by persecuting an individual, when in reality, he is doing a work for the devil.

Paul, the great Apostle, at one time was the most bitter opposer of the Christians. He held the coats of those who stoned Stephen. He was sincerely fighting for his religion, not for the GOSPEL or for GOD. His persecution of the Christians ceased when he met God on the Damascus road and found that Christ was real.

He, conversely, changed his entire life and then came his miracle ministry. Many people today are like Paul - ignorantly fighting the very Gospel the early church saints died for.

If some preachers dared, today, they would stone or destroy all ministers and saints, who by preaching against form, threaten security within traditional customs.

After Paul was delivered from their form, he preached, FROM SUCH TURN AWAY. (II Tim. 3: 5)

The prevailing opinion among Pentecostal believers is that, because they are Pentecostal in doctrine, they are RIGHT. Not so. Pentecostal believers and preachers who may have slipped from a real experience over a period of years may become bound by form and consequently cannot recognize the difference between the carnal and the spiritual. It is true that some Pentecostal church members, especially the younger generation, have grown up in the church and have never had a really personal experience with God. Usually, their religion is one of mental "assent" to a code of ethics rather than a change of heart. These are the ones that are the most bitter opposers of the genuine Pentecostal manifestations and worship in our services. Many, though they were raised in Pentecost, know nothing about old time heartfelt religion. They have never heard SHOUTS OF VICTORY, never known the joy of the Lord; never seen the sick healed, neither have they seen miracles performed and devils cast out.

These people will laugh at poor Mrs. Jones, one of the older saints that still remembers the fire falling, and criticize her for getting so "emotional" in church. All this group knows about the power of God falling, is what has been deridingly whispered to them about "holy-roller" meetings.

If there is some question about the manifestations of the Spirit, they will not go to the Bible to find out for themselves. Instead, they will ask their "dead" pastor. They will believe the church doctrine before they will believe God!

They will not have revival because it is contrary to their man-made ordinances and customs. If they fail to go along with the group in their church, they will be accused of being "disloyal" to their church. In order to

12

get along with their church, they must do everything the rest of the church does - even fight the true worshippers of Christ.

Though these church members have no power to heal the sick, or to cast out devils, or to provide deliverance for the needy themselves, they falsely accuse anyone who does have that power. Their best and only defense is to slander with words. It is much easier to say that no one else has any power and that it is all of the devil, than to start doing the works of Christ themselves.

How many of these modernists can say with Jesus, "If I do not the works of my Father, believe me not. But if I do, though ye believe not me, believe the works: that ye may know, and believe, that the Father is in me, and I in him." (John 10:37, 38) A person must have a Miracle Ministry before he can say, "IF I DO NOT THE WORKS OF MY FATHER, BELIEVE ME NOT." Jesus said, "Verily, verily, I say unto you. He that believeth on me, the works that I do shall he do also; and greater works than these shall he do; because I go unto my Father." (John 14:12)

Why does the modernist always condemn God's works instead of doing them? The answer is that he cannot do the works himself! Either because of unbelief, or because of doctrinal religious tradition, he will not permit himself to accept anything that is not written into his man-made doctrinal lines.

Why does the worst criticism always come from the dead, lifeless groups? Because this NEW RESTORATION REVIVAL is life! This is a threat to their very existence. They must fight to keep what they have. Words, slanderous words, are their only weapons with which to fight! They do not bother to back their statements with Scripture, as there is no Scripture to lend support to their claims.

It is easy for the critic to say this is not revival. I say, "If this is not revival, let some of those critics produce revival and I will get into it." Can they produce anything better? They do not really want anything other than what they have. They only want "religion" - that is what they have - religion.

The argument from the Pentecostal (so-called) churches, is that they are very Pentecostal and speak in tongues. They point at their church doctrine and constitution and say, "See, there it is. We speak in tongues. It says so."

Where is it in their church worship? There are many people who speak in tongues today, whom, I feel, no longer have the experience of the day of Pentecost. There IS MORE to receiving the Holy Ghost than

13

speaking in tongues.

The unknown tongue is only ONE of the evidences. POWER is another one. Without POWER, God given power, you may sincerely be misinformed about your experience of the baptism of the Holy Ghost!

According to Constitutional Pentecostal doctrine, you may have the real move of God; but according to your tradition, you may not have it. It is impossible for you to have a move of God while you are bound by tradition.

IN ORDER TO DEFEND THE COLDNESS and indifference in these churches, they will attack anything that is the true moving of God. Attacking the character of the one whom God is using is the first step. They said of Jesus that He was not of God but of the devil. "...

He casteth out devils through Beelzebub the chief of devils." (Luke 11:15) Some people are being deceived. God is permitting it. Why did God give lying demons permission to destroy Ahab? Because he rebelled and rejected the truth. There is every evidence that many people today, even as Ahab, are being influenced, and at times controlled, by lying demons.

Demons are as real today as they were in Bible days. "And there came forth a spirit, and stood before the Lord, and said, I will persuade him. And the Lord said unto him, Wherewith? And he said, I will go forth, and I will be a lying spirit in the mouth of all his prophets. And he said. Thou shalt persuade him, and prevail also: go forth, and do so." (I Kings 22: 21 - 22)

This demon was standing and speaking. It was a lying spirit. The object of his attack was not to attempt to cause Ahab to tell lies. His purpose was to DECEIVE Ahab with his lies.

His final objective was the destruction of Ahab, soul and body. The one objective of any demon is to LEAD or drive a soul into hell, or to cause that soul to do the thing which will be the cause of his going to hell. The prophets spoke as they were moved by A SPIRIT.

But it was not the Spirit of God.

All false doctrines and any slander against a servant of God and the moving of God's Spirit is ail or at least partially inspired by lying, satanic forces, which are designed not to lead people into the light of the truth; BUT TO BLIND THEM TO THE TRUTH and to lead them further into darkness and eventual destruction, as in the case of Ahab.

Are you associated with a group which teaches doctrinally any of the DOCTRINES OF

DEVILS? If you find that you are, do NOW exactly what the Apostle Paul commanded, "...

from such turn away." (II Tim. 3:5) In other words, WITHDRAW YOUR MEMBERSHIP.

Find yourself a church that PRACTICES all the Full Gospel. Break away now from these

"seducing spirits and doctrines of devils"!

It is dangerous to turn your back upon God's truth. When you do, you have opened the door for a lying demon, which God will then permit to come to you. "And with all deceivableness of unrighteousness in them that perish; because they received not the love of the truth, that hey might be saved. And for this cause God shall send them strong delusion, that they should believe a lie: That they all might be damned who believed not the truth, but had pleasure in unrighteousness." (II Thess. 2:10-12) Note that in the case of King Ahab, I Kings 22: 8, he had the privilege of accepting the truth. However, he rejected the truth, saying that he hated the prophet who had spoken it.

Of this prophet, a man of God named Micaiah, he said, "... but I hate him; for he doth not prophesy good concerning me, but evil ..."

This is a picture of many today who have fallen a prey to lying demons because they will not endure sound doctrine. Even as the people in days gone by, they have said, "...

Prophesy not unto us right things, speak unto us smooth things, prophesy deceits." (Isaiah 30:10)

People today are still asking for things they WANT TO HEAR, instead of the things they NEED to hear. Rejecting the truth, Ahab had Micaiah thrown into the prison, and turned for guidance to those he knew would speak pleasing flatteries. It was only after Ahab had rejected the truth that God permitted the lying spirit, through the lips of his lying prophets, to persuade Ahab to take the course which led to his death.

Ahab's prophets, inspired by the lying demon, prophesied saying, "... Go up to Ramoth-gilead, and prosper: for the Lord shall deliver it unto the king's hand." (I Kings 22:12)

Micaiah's last words to the King were,".. . If thou return at all in peace, the Lord hath not spoken by me ..." (I Kings 22: 28)

Here is one of the great Bible truths concerning demons; IT IS A DANGEROUS THING

TO REJECT GOD'S TRUTH. The moment you do, the way is open for the entrance of a LYING SPIRIT, which can come transformed as an angel of light, a messenger of God.

This demon will make you to believe a lie - and lies damn men's souls!

Lying demons have two ways of influencing people. They may speak through some other person who is yielded to their influence, as in the case of Ahab's false prophets, or they may speak directly to the person they desire to influence. This may be a matter of speaking in a voice which is (or seems to be) audible to the person they desire to influence. Often there is no sensation of an audible voice, but rather through persistent impressions, or circumstances which bear the semblance of signs.

Lying demons were quite active in Bible days. There is much evidence they are even more active today! It is their business to make people believe a lie. We are warned of this by Paul, "Now the Spirit speaketh expressly, that in the latter times some shall depart from the faith, giving heed to seducing spirits, and doctrines of devils; Speaking lies in hypocrisy; having their conscience seared with a hot iron; Forbidding to marry, and commanding to abstain from meats ..." (I Tim. 4:1-3)

"Seduce" means to lead astray: astray from God's way into Satan's way. Satan could resort to no better method than to assign seducing and lying demons to slander the real moving and manifestation of God's Spirit. No doubt, many today have rejected the truth and are believing a lie. Some are seemingly sincere in taking their stand in preaching the lies they believe.

Sincerity is not enough to prove that there is truth. A person may be sincere in believing that he is putting baking powder into pancake mixture when in reality it is Arsenic. This happened in one kitchen. A woman took a baking powder can from the top shelf in her cabinet. Arsenic was in the baking powder can. She was sincere in believing that it was powder. She fed the cakes to her entire family, only to find them all dead. She was arrested for murder. Sincerity is not enough. One must also be right. This is the danger of closing one's heart to the truth. It opens the door for STRONG DELUSION.

God permits these delusions today as surely as He did in Bible days. This is a curse from God: something that He permits to happen to those who disobey. God will permit preachers, even Pentecostal preachers to BELIEVE A LIE AND BE DAMNED.

If a person repeats a lie often enough, eventually, even he will believe that the lie is the truth. This is so because, "... God shall send them strong delusion, that they should believe a lie: That they all might be damned who believed not the truth, but had pleasure in unrighteousness." (II Thes. 2:11-12) (Insisted in having their own way, or believing what they believe, regardless of the evidence of God's Word.) Those who are deceived by these lies are as spiritually dead as Michal's womb was physically. They are as sick spiritually as Miriam was' physically. Both these women, you remember, were cursed by God for their criticism. Paul declared, "Neither murmur ye, as some of them also murmured, and were destroyed of the destroyer." (I Cor. 10:10) Did God do this? Yes. According to the Bible, GOD EVEN REJOICES OVER PEOPLE

TO DESTROY THEM and bring them to naught. "And it shall come to pass, that as the Lord rejoiced over you to do you good, and to multiply you; so the Lord will rejoice over you to destroy you, and to bring you to nought; and ye shall be plucked from off the land whither thou goest to possess it." (Deut. 28: 63) I know what God is doing today, because I know what He has done in the past. It is possible to tell what God will do in the future, because I know what He is doing now. How will God rejoice over you?

Multitudes today, because of fear, pride, form and/or tradition will take heed to lying spirits and not only believe a lie, but spread the lie they believe. They will even make it sound like the truth. In a court, with witnesses, they would shudder in their shame for spreading such slander against God and His prophets.

The pattern of lies is always the same. When you hear it, it should be a warning to close your ears. "Have you heard . . . ?" "Of course, I don't like to have to be the one to tell you about these things, but you will hear about it sooner or later. I just felt it my duty to inform you . . ." "You know I am only doing it for the sake of the Lord's work ..." Under the guise of the Lord's work, many continue doing the work of the devil. They persecuted Jesus in this manner.

"... we know that this man is a sinner." (John 9: 24) "... and a winebibber ..." (Matt. 11:19)

"... and is mad . . ." (John 10: 20) "So there was a division among the people because of him." (John 7: 43)

"... This man is not of God ..." (John 9:16) ". . .he deceiveth the people." (John 7:12) Boaster, false representative, imposter, self-made man. "... whom makest thou thyself ?"

(John 8: 53)

He is unlearned. "... How knoweth this man letters, having never learned?" (John 7:15) ". . . but by Beelzebub the prince of the devils."

(Matt. 12:24) The defense of many who believe and spread the lies of the devil is that their source is from people they call "Pentecostal". As though they are infallible, or that it is impossible for them to be misled or backslide. Paul's warning in the Bible was to the Pentecostal (no other) Church.

It is the Pentecostal Church that he was referring to which would deny the power of God and resort to a form of Godliness. The Pentecostal Church is the one which would give heed to seducing spirits.

Certainly at the time there was no Catholic, Methodist, Baptist, Presbyterian, Church of England or any other. There was only one church, the one founded on the day of Pentecost, the Pentecostal church. The warning was to the Pentecostal Church.

It would be well for the Pentecostal Church to heed the warning.

"Tongues", one evidence of the baptism of the Holy Ghost, is not enough to provide a defense of infallibility. Peter said, ". . .ye shall receive power, after that the Holy Ghost is come upon you ..." (Acts 1: 8)

In the church at Corinth, there were some ministers who were getting "puffed up" and jealous of Paul's ministry. Paul gave them a challenge that is appropriate in this our case.

These "puffed up" preachers had a great many words with which they were trying to sway the opinion of the church members. Evidently, they had gathered a number of supporters because Paul was warning the entire church in I Corinthians 4:18-20. "... and will know, not the speech of them which are puffed up, but the power. For the kingdom of God is not in word, but in power." Paul's challenge was this, "When I get there, we'll see who has the POWER".

Already, in the second chapter, Paul said that he was not coming with Excellency of speech (V. 1) but in POWER (V. 5). This Gospel is not in Debate, it is in POWER and demonstration of the Spirit.

Some preachers came to me one night after a service and wanted to challenge me to a

"public debate" on whether or not the manifestations in our services were right. I will not accept a public debate. God did not call me to argue.

In our services, we heal the sick, we cast out devils, we bring deliverance to the oppressed.

We bring light to those that sit in darkness. We cause the deaf to hear the words of the Book. Like Paul, I say, "Who's got the POWER?" Do these dead, lifeless services bring the same signs and miracles ? The

Bible declares mat THESE SIGNS shall follow them that believe. If they do not have the same signs, they do not believe. Do they have them in their services?

WHO'S GOT THE POWER?

Elijah did not take time to argue with the 400 prophets of Baal. He just wanted to know who had the power. Elijah had the power when the fire of the Lord God fell and consumed the sacrifice.

Moses did not argue with Pharaoh about whose God was greater. He just threw his rod on the floor - he just touched it into the river - Moses just parted the waters of the Red Sea.

Pharaoh found out too late, who had the power.

The children of Israel were wondering who really had the power, Aaron or the princes of the tribes. Moses did not have Aaron and the princes debate. Moses just said, "Show us who has the power." Aaron's rod budded. Aaron had the POWER!

Samson did not argue with the Philistines and tell them that they had no right to oppress his people. He just took the jawbone of an ass and showed them who had the power. I make no other defense of this ministry to dried up preachers who are bound in tradition, I just say,

"Who's got the power?"

WHO HAS THE POWER?

Two men in Acts 19 decided they would see if they had the power of God in their lives.

They did not. The devil almost destroyed them when they tried to cast it out. Perhaps those who do not have the evidenced POWER are fearful of showing whether or not they have it.

My challenge is this, "Who's got the POWER of God in their lives ?"

Satan has no reason to attack religious groups that merely have words, lies, accusations and criticism of others with which to defend their dead, powerless beliefs and denominationalism. Satan's objective is to attack the church, the group or the preacher who has the POWER or the signs, wonders and miracles in his ministry. All a man of God has to do to defend his ministry is to quote one Scripture, "... For no man can do these miracles that thou doest, except God be with him." (John 3:2) That settles the debate, does it not?

Never have any opposers to this ministry quoted John 3; 2 to prove their point. Since they cannot, they defend themselves by slander of others. Criticism will never get a miracle ministry for you. If criticism will bring anything, it will bring leprosy like it did on Miriam, the sister of Moses, after she criticized him. Beware that ye murmur not against any man.

Leprosy, which is a type of sin, may stain your wedding garment. You may never make heaven your home. It is certain that you can never see God with criticism in your heart.

The thing that disturbed the Prodigal Son's elder brother was that he heard music and dancing in his father's house. I wonder if he would walk up to your Father's house, (your church) would he be disturbed? Would he have to ask questions or would he just know what was going on since everything would be so dignified, cold and formal?

"Why," to paraphrase the servants answer, " Haven't you heard ? Your brother has come home. He who was dead is alive. He who was lost is found. Your father has killed the fatted calf and we are making merry." (Luke 15: 27) Where? In the Father's house - in the church. It was revival in the church. They were having music: the kind of music to which you dance. It must have had some rhythm. It must have had a joyful note. People do not dance to funeral music like you hear in most synagogues and churches today. This music was being played in a place where a boy had been saved. It was in a revival meeting.

Hallelujah!

The elder brother, bound by tradition said, "Humph!" He would not go into the Father's house. The Father would not let the son go away, however, "... therefore came his father out, and entreated him." (Luke 15:28) The son said, "Humph! I will not go in."

(paraphrased) Why would not the son go in ? He insisted on continuing with his tradition and he remained in bondage.

Why is Satan, or people controlled by him, so highly critical of those who enjoy the blessings of God and delight themselves in the Lord in Church? Satan does not oppose people having a good time anywhere except in the Church! Why does not Satan criticize the cold, dead, spiritless, lifeless, religious form found world widely in the denominational church? This is the reason: if he criticized the dead form, he would HAVE SCRIPTURE to back him up. The Bible declares that they have a "form of Godliness," but deny the power thereof; "... From such turn away." (II Tim. 3: 5) When Satan criticizes our shouts and rejoicing and dancing in church, why does he only use man-made philosophy and tradition to condemn it instead of Scripture? The answer is obvious. He has no Scripture with which he can condemn our worship.

Satan can only use the verbal, carnal, critical overflow from a heart that is filled with jealousy, hatred and wrath.

One Scripture which Traditionalists always use in their defense is I Kings 19:11, 12. They say that God was not in the wind, or the earthquake, or in the fire BUT - He was in the still small voice. He was in the still small voice in that ONE INSTANCE. Are these people going to limit God to moving ONLY in a still, small voice? God is a God of the lightening and the thunder as well as the still small voice.

Would these skeptics say that God is not in the wind? Would they dare say that God was not in the wind, the specific "strong east wind", that made the sea divided and the sea dry land when Moses led the children of Israel out from under the whiplash of Pharaoh's oppression? (Exodus 14: 21)

Would these skeptics be so bold as to say that God was not in the earthquake in the 16th Chapter of Numbers when God opened the earth to swallow up all those that followed in the rebellion of Korah? These modern skeptics would probably deny the fact that God, personally came down on the Mount of Sinai and caused the earth to quake. "And mount Sinai was altogether on a smoke, because the Lord descended upon it in fire: and the smoke of a furnace, and the whole mount quaked greatly." (Exodus 19:18) I would say that God was in that EARTHQUAKE. I would go so far as to say that God was responsible for the quake that caused the walls of Jericho to fall.

Would these skeptics say that God was not in the fire that came down on Mount Sinai? The Bible states, "... the Lord descended upon it in fire ..." (Exodus 19:18) In Numbers 16: 35, God was even in a FIRE that destroyed 250 people from the face of the earth!

Would the skeptic say that God was not in the fire that fell from heaven on the sacrifice of Elijah? (I Kings 18: 38) God fell on that sacrifice just to prove that HE WAS GOD! God is a GOD OF FIRE because in order to consume the sacrifice that had been soaked in water.

God had to descend from heaven in fire. Some modernistic skeptics would even say that God was not in the fire that rained from heaven on SODOM AND GOMORRAH^

(Genesis 19:24) "Then the Lord rained upon Sodom and upon Gomorrah brimstone and fire from the Lord out of heaven;" I would say that God was in fire.

Just because God was not in a wind, an earthquake and a fire ONCE, does not mean that God can never be in fire, wind or earthquakes.

21

There was even an earthquake when Christ died upon the cross for our sins. Was not God in that?

God is a GOD OF LIGHTENING AND THUNDER as well as the God of the still small voice. You say, "Well, God was not in fire in the New Testament." Tongues of fire fell on the day of Pentecost!

The skeptic will say, "What about all this noise, this shouting?" Through the entire Bible, God has admonished His people to :"Praise the Lord. . ." Psa. 147:12 "0 clap your hands . .

. shout unto God ..." Psa. 47:1 ". . . Praise God in his sanctuary ..." Psa. 150:1 "Rejoice evermore." I Thess. 5:16 " Let them praise his name in the dance ..." Psa.149:3 "Make a joyful noise unto God ..." Psa. 66; 1

The Bible encourages us to PRAISE Him, and even advises us how to praise Him and where to praise Him. We are encouraged to make a JOYFUL NOISE when we praise the Lord!

We are exhorted to CLAP OUR HANDS. We are even told to " Lift up your hands in the sanctuary . . ." Psa. 134:2 God told us to DANCE! We can LEAP, LAUGH, WEEP, SHAKE. TREMBLE, HAVE QUIVERING LIPS. FALL PROSTRATE, SPEAK IN

TONGUES, and do it all in praise to the Lord. (Write for the book, RECEIVE YE THE

HOLY GHOST which goes into detail on all the Pentecostal manifestations.) Many people today are going to miss God because they are not willing to worship God and enter into the Father's house. They are too bound by tradition. Jesus came to His own, and His own received Him not. The greatest sermon He ever preached was to the religious leaders who should have accepted Him and known Him. To them, Christ said, ". . .ye shall know the truth, and the truth shall make you free." (John 8: 32) Not one of these religious leaders was ever freed so far as we can see. They all went to hell! Why? They chose their tradition instead of the commandments of God.

It was that same group that came to Christ and said,". . . Why walk not thy disciples according to the tradition of the elders ..." (Mark 7: 5) Jesus said, "Because '. . .ye made the commandment of God of none effect by your tradition.' " (Matt. 15: 6) Tradition says,

"Well, it's in the Bible, BUT - " But what? "We'll have nothing to do with it. We don't accept it. We call it something else other than the commandments of God."

If Christ today, should come right into these churches, and the rich young ruler came running to find the way of salvation, inquiring, "... Good

Master, what shall I do that I may inherit eternal life?" (Mark 10:17) The answer that Christ gave him would cause most traditionalists to deny the ministry of Christ and say that He was begging. This is one of the greatest hindrances to revival in this country. Traditions bind the preacher until he cannot minister. Tradition blinds eyes and closes ears to the truth. "Let them alone: they be blind leaders of the blind. And if the blind lead the blind, both shall fall into the ditch."

(Matt. 15:14)

Tradition says, "You dare not say anything about money or giving in connection with the offering." Why? "The people will say you are begging." Let the devil say you are begging.

They would have said the same thing about Jesus. They do not know the commandments of God or the Word of God. Jesus was not begging in the 6th Chapter of Luke when He said,

"Give, and it shall be given unto you; good measure, pressed down, and shaken together, and running over ..." (V. 38) Was Christ begging ? No. He was ministering; healing the sick.

When the rich young ruler came to Him, inquiring the way of salvation, Jesus preached, ". . . go and sell that thou hast, and give ..." (Matt. 19: 21) People bound by tradition would scream, "Why, you are driving people away. Why don't you preach salvation instead of money ?"

The secret to this man's salvation was in money. Christ preached money, money, money, money. Why? It was a ministry and that young man's money stood between him and heaven. Jesus said, "Thou knowest the commandments . . ." (Mark 10:19) The young ruler answered,". . . All these things have I kept from my youth up: what lack I yet?" (Matt. 19:20)

Jesus had enough intestinal fortitude and enough backbone to preach a sermon on giving.

He preached on MONEY, on WEALTH. Christ did not care what the elders and the religious folk said. After Christ preached this sermon, the man left church. He went away sorrowfully because of our Lord Jesus Christ's message on giving. Christ preached giving and people went to hell because they were unwilling to give. It was not begging, but tradition today would say, it is begging for money.

The greatest sermons all the way through the Bible were the ones Jesus preached on MONEY. Yet, Christ was NOT a beggar! Why should Jesus beg when all the silver and all the gold and the cattle on a thousand hills, the earth and the fullness thereof belong to Him?

He did not have to beg for money, it was a ministry! He had to preach what God told Him to preach. "... go and sell that thou hast, and give ..." (Matt. 19:21) ". , . If any man will come after me, let him deny himself, and take up his cross, and follow me." (Matt. 16:24) A man went away grieved at the saying of the Master. The young man did not leave sorrowfully because he had money, but because he was not willing to abide by the sermon Christ preached to him. Some people would go to hell before they would give anything to God. Some people today are so bound by tradition, they will not permit their preacher to take an offering or even preach on tithes and offerings. God have mercy on that pastor, the preacher that is in such bondage that he cannot obey God and preach on giving as Jesus preached.

Ananias and Sapphira came to the First Assembly in Jerusalem and God destroyed them.

Why did God kill them? Because of money, they both died. Tradition will say, "Oh, God should not have killed Ananias and Sapphira. All they did was lie about the offering."

God has not conformed to tradition. God is doing things His way, and if you want to get in on this NEW THING God is doing today, you MUST make of none effect, destroy all the traditions of men in order to get into it.

Was God angry because He did not get all of Ananias and Sapphira's money? No! God did not need their money. They decided to give it. God killed them because IT IS SIN TO

DISOBEY the voice of God when He speaks.

Preaching on giving can be a ministry from God. The rich young ruler could have "given"

his way into heaven. Ananias and Sapphira "gave their way into hell" with a wrong attitude in their giving. If they had received more preaching on GIVING with the right objective, they might have been saved.

Was Elijah after the widow's last cake when he asked her to ". . . make me thereof a little cake first ..." (I Kings 17:13) Was he a charlatan when he said, "... and after make for thee and for thy son." (V. 13) Was he a false prophet when he continued, "For thus saith the Lord God of Israel, The barrel of meal shall not waste, neither shall the cruse of oil fail, until the day that the Lord sendeth rain upon the earth." (V. 14) He was none of these.

Neither was he a beggar.

Elijah was a man with a ministry. He was sent of God to deliver the

24

widow from the demon of poverty and bestow upon her the blessing of prosperity. Would he have been free to preach such a sermon in the average pulpit today? No!

First of all, the deacons would not let him. Secondly, he would be afraid, because of tradition, that the congregation would say that he was just out for money. He might even fear that the congregation would get up and walk out of his service. In light of all this, would he go along with tradition, not only concerning tithes and offerings, but also in every phase of doctrine and form of worship ?

He would be confined ONLY TO THAT WHICH WAS APPROVED BY THE ELDERS

OR THE HEADS OF HIS DENOMINATION. How impossible it would be under these circumstances for God to do a new thing for him. He would never know Revival. God would never do a new thing in his life. The pattern for his life and ministry would have been set down in a book written by a man who has been left out of the NEW

RESTORATION REVIVAL.

If revival ever comes to the world, preaching on money (or at least my preaching on money) will have to be considered a ministry instead of begging. God has given me a ministry. We never BEG for money. This is a ministry. God has promised, ". . . it is he that giveth thee power to get wealth ..." (Deut. 8:18) When John said, under the inspiration of the Spirit of God, "Beloved, I wish above all things that thou mayest prosper and be in health . . ." (Ill John 1:2)

He was not begging for the people's money. He was telling them that it was God's will for them to prosper financially as well as physically.

When Job declared, "Then shalt thou lay up gold as dust, and the gold of Ophir as the stones of the brooks . . . and thou shalt have plenty of silver . . . and thou shalt pay thy vows." (Job 22:24, 25, 27) Job was not begging for money. He was trying to show you that, you too can prosper. He did not need anything. He was trying to show people the reason they did not have any money: they would not pay their vows. In the 50th Psalm, verse 14, David said, "Offer unto God thanksgiving; and pay . . ."

David was not after money. He had money: rooms full of it! He was one of the richest men of his time. David was not out for money when he said, "... pay thy vows . . ." (V. 14) It was a ministry. David was not begging. It was something straight from heaven because the people needed it in order to be delivered from their troubles.

"... pay thy vows unto the most High: And call upon me in the day of trouble; I will deliver thee, and thou shalt glorify me." (Psa. 50:14, 15) The tradition of the elders, that nullifies the commandments of God and the Word of God, would say, " Listen to David begging for money. He's just out for the money." Many ministers let this same tradition bind them until they will not preach on tithes and offerings. Is it any wonder that they have to sell insurance or automobiles or be a carpenter in order to support themselves in the Gospel ?

In the 76th Psalm, verse 11, the power of God came upon David and he said, "Vow, and pay unto the Lord your God: let all that be round about him bring presents unto him that ought to be feared." Today's traditionally bound congregation would hiss, "Listen to David: taking pledges again. I don't believe in taking pledges."

Why not? It is the Word of God and it is a Commandment of God. "Vow!" Make a vow and pay that vow! Job said, "Then shalt thou lay up gold as dust ... (if you want prosperity) pay thy vows." (Job 22:24, 25, 27)

According to David, deliverance from your troubles has a direct connection in paying something to God. How can a person say, "I do not believe in making pledges," when God said, "Vow, and pay unto the Lord your God . . ." (Psa. 76:11) Tradition, today, tells people that preachers have no business saying, "Vow and pay!"

David said it and he was not begging for money. He was telling everyone that it was a ministry and if they want God's blessing, they must bring presents unto Him. You must vow and pay that vow.

Tradition will so bind preachers that they cannot do the will of God, but must do according to the will of the elders. They cannot do according to Peter and Paul, David and Job.

In the 18th Chapter of Deuteronomy, Moses preached one of the greatest sermons ever preached. He would not be free, however, to preach it in some of these churches today.

Tradition would prohibit it. Tradition has the people so bound, they would all get up and walk out of his service. As one pastor from Finland told me, "Now, remember one thing.

You dare not say anything about money, or offerings. You dare not say anything about giving or money in connection with the offering." He continued, "One evangelist came in to hold meetings and said something about offerings. Brother Allen, many people got up and left him." I said, "Do you mean that I cannot come to Finland and preach the Gospel?"

"Oh," he replied, "Yes, do preach the Gospel." I said, "Under those circumstances, if Jesus had come to your meeting, and a man similar to the rich young ruler in Luke 18 would come to the altar and ask, 'What must I do to inherit eternal life ?' would Jesus be permitted to answer him?" Jesus would have had to say, "Well, now, I'm sorry, I cannot tell you what to do to inherit eternal life because I'm so bound by tradition that I cannot preach on giving and it is your money that is standing between you and heaven. But, alas, I cannot show you the way to heaven."

"Well, preach it!" said the pastor. "But do not preach it in connection with taking an offering. Preach it some other time and let someone else sing, preach and then take the offering."

He explained that when another evangelist was there on a previous campaign, a certain Pentecostal newspaper in Finland, printed lies concerning the offerings. The Pentecostal paper, staying in tradition, printed that he and this evangelist from America were out to get all the money they could and then they would split it 50 - 50.

The pastor assured me that it was the biggest lie ever printed. Even though it came through a Pentecostal newspaper, it was still an untruth. This proves that even Pentecostal people, preachers, laity, so-called saints and religious periodicals are so bound by tradition that if an Evangelist does something a little different than their tradition, they will brand him as being out for money and will accuse him of splitting it with the pastor. This condition prevails not only in Finland but exists all over the world.

God help so-called Pentecostal people who are so bound by this tradition. The worst skeptics are the so-called Pentecostal people that have a form of Godliness denying the power thereof! Referring to them, Paul said, "... from such turn away." (II Tim. 3; 5) Before Revival can come, the church, YOU, must break away from these traditions of men.

They nullify, make of none effect the Word of God and the commandments of God.

Jesus came to His own and His own received Him not. He preached the truth, they would not receive it. They murdered Christ! They called Him a devil, casting out devils by the power of Beelzebub. They called Him everything, including a winebibber. They called Him all these things BECAUSE He had broken away from and failed to conform to the tradition of the elders. For this reason, Christ was crucified. For this reason. His apostles and disciples died a violent death at the hands of Religious Leaders. Thank God they would not conform to the tradition of the elders.

Moses had a ministry! He also began to preach the blessing of prosperity. He would dare not preach it in some of these churches today.

Traditions would brand him a fraud. Moses preached, POWER TO GET WEALTH. (Deut. 8:18) I preach the same sermon.

There is a power to cast out devils. There is a power to heal the sick. There is a power to lay hands on people and bestow every heavenly blessing. We lay our hands on people and thousands of people receive the Holy Ghost in a single service. However, if I had never denounced the traditions of my denomination that I was a part of for 25 years, we would not be having the revival we are having today. In order to have revival, we must believe the commandments of God and keep them.

Tradition nullifies and makes of none effect the commandments of God. This is why you find so many cold, dead, dry, formal church people, I will confess that they are religious, but they do not know the moving of the Spirit or the reality of the anointing of God. Many of them have never felt the power of God. If they have, they have been afraid to let it do anything for them: afraid that somebody will brand them as being "super-spiritual", "emotionalist", being a "fanatic", in the "flesh", of the"devil", being "sensational", or becoming "hysterical" !

Moses spent forty days with God on the Mount Sinai. When he came down from the mountain, his face was shining with God's glory so much that the people could not even look at him. Moses did not begin to tell them of what a wonderful meeting with God he had experienced. God had spoken to Moses, telling him to return to the people and tell them to bring God an offering.

The first thing Moses did was to take an offering. He was not backslidden either. He had been fasting and praying: talking to God. Tradition would not let him take an offering today. Tradition would say he had backslidden up on the mountain and was just out to get money. According to the Word of God, however, he had been talking with God. He was under the anointing of the Spirit of God so completely that his face was shining brightly and had to be covered up. In all this glory, in the midst of this great move of God, the first thing Moses did was to take an offering.

Still under the inspiration, Moses gave us the 8th Chapter: "When thou hast eaten and art full, then thou shalt bless the Lord thy God for the good land which he hath given thee.

Beware that thou forget not the Lord thy God, in not keeping his commandments, and his judgments, and his statutes, which I command thee this day: Lest when thou hast eaten and art full, and hast built goodly houses, and dwelt therein; And when thy herds and thy flocks multiply, and thy silver and thy gold is multiplied; Then thine heart be lifted up, and thou forget the Lord thy God, which brought thee forth . . . And thou say in thine heart. My power (meaning my own power, ingenuity, ability, wisdom, knowledge or talent) and the might of mine hand (own physical strength) hath gotten me this wealth (this paycheck or this income)." Was Moses begging OR do you believe that he had a ministry?

"But thou shalt remember the Lord thy God: for it is he that giveth thee power to get wealth . . ." (Deut. 8:18) Moses preached that there was a power from heaven that enabled God's children to prosper and be wealthy so that they could have money to give for the Glory of God. It takes money to preach the Gospel. Christ cannot return until this has been preached. If the Gospel could be preached free, Christ would have come a long time ago.

It will take millions of dollars to take this Gospel, as we are preaching it, around the world.

Tradition would never allow Moses to preach this sermon today. Yet, there is a power that comes from God that enables people to get wealth. God will enable you to be wealthy.

Tradition would say, "Moses is just out to deceive the people. It's a fraud. He is just out trying to make them think they can't have wealth or prosperity unless God gives them peculiar powers."

Contrary to what tradition will say, Moses did have a ministry and he was under the inspiration of the Spirit of God. When we preach "Power to Get Wealth", we are not preaching for money, we preach this for your help and benefit. Other preachers would like to preach this also, but they cannot.

Preachers are too bound by the tradition of the elders to preach this sermon. If they did, the elders would take away their ordination papers, or their credentials and kick them out of the denomination. If revival ever comes to your country, it will be because the traditions become nil and of none effect INSTEAD of the commandments of God becoming nullified and of none effect.

We must break away from, be delivered from, the religious tradition of the elders.

According to Scripture, some will never be delivered because they have been nullifying and destroying God's Word for too many years. Literally, they are dead to the Word of God. "Having the understanding darkened, being alienated from the life of God through the ignorance that is in them, because of the blindness of their heart." (Eph. 4:18) Some of these people will never come out of their darkness. They will never wake up. If you were to have an operation at the hospital, you would first be given an anesthetic to nullify the pain: so you would not feel the pain. The pain is there, you just cannot feel it.

You have been made "dead".

When you come to your full senses, then you begin to feel the pain. When the nullifying effect of the drug wears off, then you begin to hurt. That is when they will administer another pill or shot in the arm. Why? To keep your body "dead", or insensate to pain.

Offtimes, when a surgeon operates on your extremities, you will be given just one shot in the spine. That is called a "spinal". Sometimes that "spinal" has a permanent nullifying effect on the body. Many people that are brought into our meetings have had a spinal and are paralyzed from the waist down and can feel nothing. Pins can be stuck into their legs and they will feel no pain. They have been "nullified". They will never feel anything without a miracle from God.

Many people today have not been given a spinal, but they have had an injection, not from God, into their hearts. They will never feel the commandments of God, the Spirit of God, or the power of God because they have been dead and nullified too long by following the tradition of men. There is little hope for people who are so cold and dead. They have no feeling - they never will.

After a long period of time, the tradition makes you completely lifeless. There was no hope for the Pharisees and Sadducees. They felt nothing. When the disciples came into Jerusalem shouting of all the miracles they had seen, the Pharisees and Sadducees said, "...

Master, rebuke thy disciples." (Luke 19: 39) Jesus replied saying that He would not rebuke them. ". . .1 tell you that, if these should hold their peace, the stones would immediately cry out." (Luke 19:40)

The elder brother was so nullified that he never came to life. He asked, "What are these things?" (paraphrasing) "IT'S REVIVAL!" "I don't like all this music and dancing."

Yet, they kept dancing and playing the music. They just left him on the outside. Friend, you had better be careful of your criticism of the moving of God's power. Some people will be left on the outside. Your tradition, which makes of none effect the commandments of God, will keep you from being blessed and prospered.

Tradition will keep you from the manifestations of the Spirit. It will keep you from the baptism of the Holy Ghost and the gifts of the

Spirit. It will keep you from giving to God.

Some are so bound that they cannot raise their hands. Raising hands is one of the least of the manifestations of the Spirit.

The Bible declares, "... lifting up holy hands ..." (I Tim. 2: 8) It is written, "0 clap your hands, all ye people; shout unto God with the voice of triumph." (Psa. 47:1) "Let everything that hath breath praise the Lord..." (Psa. 150: 6) Solomon said, "To every thing there is a season, and a time to every purpose under the heaven." (Ecclesiastes 3:1) There is a time to dance. David said, "Let them praise his name in the dance ..." (Psa. 149: 3) Dance? "Well, that's altogether different." No, there is no difference! For the same man that said for us to clap our hands, shout, and praise Him on the organs also said, "Praise Him in the dance!" (paraphrased) Tradition will say, "I know it's in the Bible, BUT. . . " Those people are so bound by tradition, by the elders, that they will just stay bound. Be careful that you do not stay bound too long. You may miss the rapture!

If you are bound by one thing, it may as well be the worst sin mentioned in the Bible. If you are bound by one thing, you are no better off than people that are bound by something else. Some people are bound by Liquor! Some are bound by narcotics, tobacco or one demon or another. Others are bound by tradition. Tradition will bring you in from the field to the Father's house to say, "What is all this going on? I don't understand what's going on!"

Tradition will make you sit like Michal and say, "Humph! How glorious was the King today in front of all the handmaids!" Tradition will tell Jesus to rebuke His disciples.

However, when you break away from tradition, you will say, "Leave them ALONE." You may as well say it. Why don't you join us? Some say., "Well, if God ever makes me dance, I will." If you LET God: He will. Most worshippers are stiff and unyielding to God.

Have you ever gone window shopping; ? Looking in the big glass windows, you will see a man standing and/or a woman sitting. Really, it is not a man, neither is it a woman. It does look like a man or woman though. Many church people LOOK real, but they are so dead and lifeless that they cannot be real. They are just as lifeless, unyielded, dead and spiritless, as the mannequin in the store window made out of plaster of Paris.

God has never made one of those mannequins dance. I have never heard of one of them clapping their hands, or shouting, singing or praising the Lord. They never do any worshipping of God, because God DOES

NOT MAKE THEM DO IT. Neither will He MAKE you praise Him!

People, church people, who never worship God in the manifestations of the Spirit, have been nullified on the inside. They are dead on the inside. There is nothing within them that is capable of yielding to God. Many church people will remain DEAD, unless God performs a miracle. It will have to be the same type of miracle that Christ performed when He walked up to the tomb of Lazarus and said,". . . Lazarus, come forth." (John 11; 43) Lazarus was lifeless, cold, dead and nullified to everything (like many people today).

When Jesus spoke, Lazarus began to come to life. He came out of bondage and captivity.

Jesus said, "... Loose him, and let him go." (John 11: 44) If you are in a cold, lifeless church, if you are still listening to the tradition of the elders and if you do not have the manifestations of the Spirit in your worship, YOU NEED A MIRACLE OF RESURRECTION IN YOUR LIFE.

In faith, I am going to pray what I call a PRAYER OF DELIVERANCE for you that read this book. I have prayed this prayer for thousands of people around the world. Many would be in hell at this moment if I had not prayed this prayer for them. This prayer will not save you, for only the BLOOD OF JESUS can cleanse from sin. I do not claim to have power to save (I never have and never will), but one thing I do claim and that is POWER OVER

THE DEVIL.

As you read this prayer, read it in a LOUD voice and believe that God will loose you and let you go free.

NOW FATHER,I PRAY IN THE NAME OF JESUS, THAT YOU LOOSE EVERY

YOKE ON THIS PERSON. I COMMAND YOU, SATAN, BY THE POWER THAT

WORKETH IN ME, TO LET THIS PERSON GO FREE. I COMMAND THAT THE JOY

OF THE LORD RETURN. -I COMMAND THAT THE OIL OF JOY BE GIVEN FOR

THIS SPIRIT OF MOURNING. I COMMAND THAT THE GARMENTS OF PRAISE

BE GIVEN FOR THIS SPIRIT OF HEAVINESS, I COMMAND THIS IN THE NAME

OF JESUS.. AMEN.

www.ingramcontent.com/pod-product-compliance
Lightning Source LLC
Chambersburg PA
CBHW030010040426
42337CB00012BA/726